DATE

MYRA BRADWELL
First Woman Lawyer

Notable Americans

MYRA BRADWELL
First Woman Lawyer

Elizabeth Wheaton

MORGAN
REYNOLDS
Incorporated

Greensboro

MYRA BRADWELL *First Woman Lawyer*

Photo credits: cover, pp. 19, 27, 51, Chicago Historical Society; pp. 29, 45, 83, Chicago
Public Library; p. 39, Cincinnati Historical Society; pp. 81, 85, Illinois Historical Society;
pp. 57, 65, 75, Library of Congress.

Library of Congress Cataloging-in-Publication Data
Wheaton, Elizabeth
  Myra Bradwell, first woman lawyer / Elizabeth Wheaton. — 1st ed.
     p. cm. — (Notable Americans)
  Includes bibliographical references and index.
  Summary: Recounts the life of Myra Bradwell, the nineteenth-century activist, newspaper
publisher, businesswoman, and lawyer.
  ISBN 1-883846-17-X (hardcover)
     1. Bradwell, Myra, 1831-1894—Juvenile literature. 2. Women lawyers—Illinois—
Chicago—Biography—Juvenile literature. 3. Women's rights—United States—History—
19th century—Juvenile literature. [1. Bradwell, Myra, 1831-1894. 2. Lawyers.
3. Women—biography] I. Title II. Series.
KF368. B712W48 1997
340'.092—dc21
[B]

                                              96-37082
                                                   CIP

Printed in the United States of America

First Edition

For Kelley and Sam

CONTENTS

Chapter One

Abolitionist Childhood

Myra Colby was six years old when Elijah Lovejoy, a friend of her parents, was murdered by a mob enraged by the anti-slavery editorials he published in his newspapers in St. Louis, Missouri and Alton, Illinois. Elijah Lovejoy's friendship with the Colbys was based on their mutual hatred of slavery. After their friend's murder, Eben and Abigail Colby increased their involvement in the abolition movement.

Young Myra watched her parents suffer through the loss of their friend and re-dedicate themselves to the cause of ending slavery. She vowed to grow up and devote her life to fighting for what she knew was right. That's what her family had always done. One ancestor, Samuel Chase, had signed the Declaration of Independence, and a relative, Salmon P. Chase, was a politician who helped lead the fight against slavery. After the Civil War, he would be sitting on the U.S. Supreme Court when Myra appealed for her right to practice law.

Myra, who was the Colby's fifth and final child, was born on February 12, 1831, in Manchester, Vermont, but her family moved to the Genessee River Valley south of Rochester, New York, when she was a year old. The valley was more fertile than the foothills of Vermont and was in the heart of "The Burned-over District," a region that "blazed" with religious revivals which focused on the evils of slavery. In this atmosphere a girl like Myra could not help but learn that it was not only her right—it was her duty—to try to change laws that were wrong.

In 1843, when Myra was twelve, the Colby family moved again, this time to Illinois, the edge of the western frontier.

Hundreds of families from New York's Burned-over District had migrated west since the 1830s, and the letters they wrote made the vast prairies sound like the Garden of Eden. The land was flat, the soil was rich and easy to plow, and game was plentiful. Rivers and streams criss-crossed the state, feeding lush hardwood groves—some large enough to shelter a settlement, others just the right size for a farmhouse.

There was another reason for the large migration from the Burned-over District to the Illinois frontier. The religious revivals inspired thousands to become missionaries who often moved west in groups of twenty or thirty families to form a ready-made colony. These fellowships were united in their belief that slavery must be actively opposed.

For many, this meant moving to areas bordering on slave states where they could provide direct assistance to escaped slaves, such as helping with the dangerous task of moving fugitives along the secret escape route called the Underground Railroad to the fast-growing port of Chicago, where ships would take them to freedom in Canada.

The Colbys chose to settle near Elgin, a lush region of dairy farms on the Fox River about thirty-five miles northwest of Chicago. Although it was off the main route of the Underground Railroad, Elgin had a small network of "conductors" and supporters who provided safehouses, food and clothing, and transportation either to Chicago or north along the Fox River to Wisconsin.

Myra was excited about heading for the frontier. But moving a household in the 1840s was not an easy task. They traveled by wagon and had to carry enough provisions to last the entire trip. That meant they would have to leave all but their most essential belongings behind. Making those choices about her own things—clothes, books, dolls, pets—was difficult for Myra. She also had to say good-bye to her friends and schoolmates, which always makes the heart ache.

The Colbys left New York as soon as it looked like the spring rains had passed, to avoid getting bogged down on muddy wagon trails. They traveled with a few other families to help each other out in case of accident or injury. Even under the best weather conditions, the trails were full of ruts, rocks and tree stumps which could break a wheel, an axle, or a horse's leg.

Usually the men and older boys led the wagons on foot, leaving the women and small children to bounce along inside. But Myra, being Myra, was not content to sit in a wagon which rattled her bones and teeth all day. She took the reins and guided the horses from the driver's seat, or sometimes she drove from the comfort of one of the horses' broad backs or walked between the pair, a set of reins in each hand.

The Colbys were exhausted when they reached their new home. Neighbors and fellow abolitionists helped them settle in, and soon life returned to normal.

Among the Colbys' regular visitors in their new home was Owen Lovejoy, Elijah's brother, who lived in Princeton, Illinois, but traveled extensively as a Congregational minister and a leader in the Underground Railroad.

While most members of the underground were highly secretive about their work, Owen went so far as to advertise in the *Western Citizen*, an abolitionist newspaper. His ad told "ladies and gentlemen of color, who wish to travel North for the benefit of their condition" that he would provide them with free transportation, clothes and food. He invited them to "inquire at his residence" at any hour.

Although Illinois was a free state, search parties and bounty hunters often tracked runaways far into neighboring northern states. Anyone found harboring slaves could be

Owen Lovejoy was a leader in the Underground Railroad.

arrested and prosecuted—if the searchers did not enact their own "vigilante justice" first.

Owen Lovejoy and his family were threatened many times, and he was prosecuted at least once. But by casting himself in the spotlight, he drew attention away from others, thereby allowing them to continue their work in secrecy.

Myra's independent spirit and energetic nature blossomed in this atmosphere. In later life she often remembered Owen Lovejoy and spoke of his influence on her. His stories about Elijah's martyrdom, about his own abolition work and his growing sense that this would become a political battle, and especially about the crucial role of a free press as an instigator of social change—all had a profound effect on Myra.

Her discussions with Owen provided the model for Myra's adult life, but she still needed an education. As many advantages as there were to living in Illinois, one serious drawback was that there were no public schools in the 1840s. The Colbys sent Myra to Kenosha, Wisconsin, to live with her now-married sister Abbie and to attend a private girl's school.

Private schools provided an education in language, literature and the arts. In addition, most girl's schools were designed to teach the proper role of women in society. According to this philosophy, only men were trained for leadership roles, whether in church, business, politics, or the family. God and nature had ordained women to embody four virtues: piety, purity, submissiveness, and domesticity. Or, as one male writer of the day put it: "So long as she is nervous, fickle, capricious, delicate, diffident, and dependent, men will worship and adore her. Her weakness is her strength, and her true art is to cultivate and improve that weakness."

Myra had no problem with piety, nor with purity or domesticity. But submissiveness? Weakness? Slaves were expected to be submissive, and Myra knew that was wrong. Why should it be any different for women?

Chapter Two

Civil War Years

Myra returned to the Colby home in 1851 to complete her studies at the newly opened Elgin Seminary for Females. She had decided to become a teacher, one of the few jobs open to women.

To most women of Myra's age and social class, education beyond high school, and work outside the home, were not attractive options. Their first concern was to marry into a family of at least equal, but preferably higher, social status. To that end, parties and receptions were a must for the sons and daughters of the area's most prosperous landowners and businessmen.

With her dark good looks, her intellect and sense of humor, and her irrepressible spirit, Myra quickly became "the acknowledged belle of Elgin." To her escorts and their parents, she was the ideal candidate for marriage. Myra seemed destined for a marriage into a prestigious local family.

Myra had other plans. Soon after entering the seminary,

she met James Bradwell. James had no money and no social standing—his parents were English immigrants who had a small farm near Palatine, about twenty miles northeast of Elgin. But, lean and muscular at six-foot-two, James was a handsome and imposing sight. Like Myra, he had spirit and ambition. More important to Myra, he cherished her independence as much as she did. She knew James was her soul mate, but her parents refused to give up their hopes of Myra marrying a wealthier, better-established man.

When Myra and James met, he was working as a skilled laborer and studying law at night. He had worked his way through Knox Manual Labor College, which, despite its name, was not a training school for tradesmen. Knox College was founded in Galesburg in the 1830s. It was modeled on New York's Oneida Institute and Ohio's Oberlin College and borrowed their philosophy that higher education should groom its students into well-rounded citizens who found spiritual meaning in manual skill as well as in academic achievement. All students—not just needy students like James—were required to spend part of each day working on campus upkeep and repair. Other components of the school's philosophy were abolition of slavery and women's equality.

As much as the Colbys agreed with James's social values, they were opposed to their daughter being courted by a pauper. There was even a story that Myra's brother Frank, by then a lawyer, once chased James off the property with a shotgun. Only Abbie supported Myra, and she was far away in Kenosha.

Most young women would have bowed to their parents' wishes. For that matter, most young men would have beaten a hasty retreat after being threatened with a shotgun. But Myra and James were not like most others. On May 18, 1852, they eloped to Chicago.

A few months after their marriage, the newlyweds moved to Memphis, Tennessee, where they opened a small private school. James continued his legal studies and later that year took his bar exam and was admitted to the Tennessee bar.

Although the school they started was highly respected and quite successful, Myra and James decided to move to Chicago after their second year in Memphis. They disliked living in a slave state.

The birth of her first child, a daughter named Myra, softened the attitude of the Colbys toward the marriage. Soon after James was admitted to the Illinois bar, he and Myra's brother Frank formed a law partnership. The firm of Bradwell & Colby was created in 1855 and quickly became a success.

Chicago of the late 1850s was fast becoming the Midwestern center of commerce and industry. With its port, its growing rail lines, its boat canal running all the way to the Mississippi at St. Louis, and the sprouting of telegraph lines from city to city, Chicago grew from 30,000 population in

As a young woman Myra was the "acknowledged belle of Elgin."

1850 to 112,000 in 1860.

Myra and James thrived in the fast-paced life the city offered. They were active in community affairs—political, charitable, and social. They knew the city's movers and shakers and impressed them with their energy and their bright minds.

James developed an excellent reputation, both for his outstanding legal work and for his "natural gifts as an eloquent and forceful speaker." In 1861 the people of Chicago and surrounding Cook County elected him to be a judge on the county probate court. He was soon regarded as an expert in wills and estate administration.

During the years before the Civil War, two more children were born to the Bradwells: Thomas, in 1856, and Bessie, in 1858.

The Civil War, a tragedy for the nation, started in 1861. That same year brought grief to the Bradwell family when little Myra died. She was seven years old. Then, in 1862, a son they named James was born, but he lived only two years. The cause of their deaths is not known, but epidemics of typhoid and cholera, bred by the open sewage that ran into the Chicago River, were common occurrences during the war years when thousands of troops converged on cities ill-equipped to handle the rapid population increases. President Lincoln's son Willie died of a similar disease in 1862.

Despite the agony of losing two children the Bradwells, like most Americans, worked for a Union victory during the war years. Myra helped found and became president of the Chicago Soldiers' Aid Society, an organization that made clothing and bandages for the Union Army and raised money to support wounded soldiers and their families.

New Year's Day of 1863 brought an event Myra had waited for since birth. The Emancipation Proclamation freed the slaves held in the territory of the Confederacy. The announcement of the act brought uproarious celebrations, even though it was not a complete victory for the abolitionist cause.

The war raged on. The Union forces were far superior—in men, arms, and supplies—but the Confederates were determined and continued to take a heavy toll on the U.S. troops in battle after battle. Throughout the northern states, women intensified their work. Sanitary commissions inspected and worked to improve conditions at army hospitals and homes for disabled soldiers. In 1863 these commissions joined forces with groups like the Chicago Soldiers' Aid Society and organized fund-raising events called sanitary fairs.

In Chicago, hundreds of volunteers, including Myra and suffragist Mary Livermore, created exhibits and displays for the Northwest Sanitary Fair. They also recruited speakers, among them was the old Colby family friend Owen Lovejoy, who was then serving his second term in Congress. Lovejoy was in poor health. Gaunt from bouts of liver and kidney failure, and against his doctor's orders, he made the long journey to Chicago. He would not let Myra down.

There were thousands in the audience when Owen took the podium, and he did not disappoint them. Summoning strength from the depth of his soul, Owen's voice boomed across the fairground: "Do not let any power from earth or from beneath the earth alienate your attachment or weaken your confidence in the President."

He was a grand orator, hushing the crowd with awe, bringing them to their feet with cheers, punching the air with his fist to emphasize a point. He concluded with the message that had been his passion for twenty-six years: "And now let the people in their sovereignty and power, through their chosen representatives in Congress, complete what has so auspiciously begun, and pass an act of universal emancipation, and thus make Union and liberty now and forever one and inseparable."

It was Owen Lovejoy's last public speech. He lived to see his beloved President re-elected to his second term. Had he been strong enough, Owen would have cheered Lincoln's inaugural address, which he could have written himself. On learning of Owen's death in March 1864, Lincoln said, "Lovejoy was the best friend I had in Congress."

In the last months of the war, Myra organized the largest sanitary fair. There were two major exhibit spaces, one at the courthouse, the other at an ornate hall which later became the Grand Opera House. The fair was a huge success, raising $70,000 for war relief.

After the fair Myra received much of the credit for its success. "Mrs. Judge Bradwell," as the *Voice of the Fair*, the event's official publication, reported, "devoted all her wonderful energies to its complete success; her attentiveness to everybody and everything have been unceasing, and in the midst of a melange of questions which would have frenzied an ordinary person, her courtesy and kindness have maintained an equable glow. The flattering success of this department must, to a vast extent, be attributed to her connection with it."

Women's experiences in efforts like the sanitary fairs and the Soldiers' Aid Society, as well as in supporting their families while their husbands and fathers were at war, opened their eyes to their potential as full members of American society. They had been brought up to believe that they were physically and mentally incapable of anything more than housework and motherhood. The war taught women that they could run households and farms, churches and schools; work in the fields and in the factories; manage civic and charitable organizations; raise money and recruit volunteers. Thousands of women learned to fight for what they believed in and to be proud of their success. The women the Civil War veterans came home to were not the women they left behind. The "Second Civil War," the "Quiet Civil War," had begun.

Chapter Three

Chicago Legal News

In the years before the Civil War, Myra worked regularly with James in his law practice. Marriage, to them, was much more than a home-based relationship. As Myra told one reporter, "I believe that married people should share the same toil and the same interests and should be separated in no way. It is the separation of interests and labor that develops people in opposite directions and makes them grow apart. If they worked side by side and thought side by side, we would need no divorce courts."

While that philosophy might not work for everyone, for Myra and James it forged an everlasting bond. And, true to their characters, it worked both ways.

Two crucial developments grew out of their work together. First, it soon became obvious that Myra could develop into as capable a lawyer as James. And second, they realized that it was almost impossible to be an effective lawyer without access to the recent higher court rulings and to the new laws enacted by the state legislature. At the time, months might pass before such crucial information was made available to practicing attorneys.

Myra decided to begin studying the law, with James as her tutor. They also discussed starting a weekly newspaper to bring lawyers timely information about legal developments. But the advent of the war forced them to put their plans aside.

At the Civil War's end, Myra began studying for the bar exam in earnest. Lawyers at that time were not required to be law school graduates. They had to have sufficient knowledge of the law to pass a written examination, and take oral examinations before the state Supreme Court, which would then accept—or reject—them to practice law.

Although no women had yet taken, much less passed, a bar examination in the United States, Myra was determined to be the first. James guided her studies, and her knowledge and her proficiency grew. She was confident of success.

Her acceptance by the Supreme Court seemed equally assured. They were personal friends of Justice Sidney J. Breese and knew the other members of the Court professionally. The only thing standing in her way was the prejudice against women practicing law. Surely, after the experience of the war, she wouldn't be denied the opportunity solely because of her sex. There was a great deal of work to be done before she was ready to take the bar exam. In the meantime, Myra found other outlets for her energy.

Myra continued to devote time to charitable activities. When the Soldiers' Home had outlived its original purpose, she helped establish the Illinois Industrial School for Girls at the site.

In 1866 Myra and James discovered a young couple who shared their energy, their ideals, and their commitment to legal reform. Like James, Catharine and Charles Waite had also attended Knox College in the 1840s. Charles was a lawyer, although before the war he was publisher of an anti-slavery newspaper in Rock Island, Illinois. In 1862, at the request of President Lincoln, he and Catharine moved to the Utah Territory where he served as Associate Justice of the Utah Supreme Court.

Catharine Waite was as opinionated and outspoken as Myra Bradwell. While in Utah she minced no words in her opposition to the Mormon practice of polygamy—a man taking multiple wives. What started out as a "cordial" reception among the settlers soon turned hostile. A year later the Waites moved to Idaho where Charles started a law practice and began to dabble in politics. But the couple missed Chicago and decided to return in 1866.

Catharine was thirty-seven, Charles was forty-three, and they had five children when they met the Bradwells. Despite her age, Catherine wanted to become a doctor. She applied to Chicago's Rush Medical College and was rejected. Although women had reluctantly been allowed into the medical profession during the war, the returning veterans

James Bradwell became one of Chicago's best known attorneys.

quickly re-established their exclusive claims to jobs and education. Catharine decided to channel her personal disappointment into political action.

The Waites and the Bradwells were a well-matched team. Mary Livermore, Myra's colleague from the sanitary fairs, also became a member of their close-knit group, and soon Illinois had a small but dynamic women's rights brigade. They talked, they brainstormed, and they organized—the men participating as eagerly as the women.

They knew from their experience with the abolition movement that it was important for them to join in with a national organization. They decided to work with the National Woman Suffrage Association, led by Susan B. Anthony and Elizabeth Cady Stanton.

Charles Waite, the former newspaper publisher, encouraged Myra in her plans to start a publishing company. Myra and James knew it would be a tremendously expensive venture. Because Myra wanted to run a general printing operation to supply lawyers with legal forms, stationery, and books updating legal statutes, as well as publish a weekly legal newspaper, she would need to have an entire factory.

There was another matter that the Bradwells had to deal with before Myra could start the presses rolling. This hurdle was a test of their political influence. As a married woman, Myra was legally prohibited from running a business in her name. Many married couples got around the law by having

Myra and James worked to improve the image of the Cook County Courthouse.

the husband's name listed as the company president and having him sign all the legal and financial papers necessary for day-to-day business.

The Bradwells did not think that skirting the law was a valid option. The Illinois legislature enacted thousands of bills each year that made special provisions for corporations that would otherwise have been prohibited from doing business in the state. Myra and James had no doubt that their newspaper, publishing news of changes in the law throughout the state, was much needed by lawyers and businessmen, as well as the legislators themselves. They decided to ask the legislature to give Myra permission to own the corporation.

They began building support by talking with their legal and business contacts in Chicago. They also lobbied legislators. All they needed was one lawmaker to sponsor a bill and a few more to support it in the House and Senate.

Eventually, their efforts were rewarded and, by special act of the Illinois legislature, Myra was given complete legal authority to establish and run in her name the Chicago Legal News Company and its weekly publication, the *Chicago Legal News*. On October 3, 1868, the premier edition hit the street. It was an immediate success and quickly established itself as "the most important legal publication west of the Alleghenies."

The Bradwells scored another victory in the legislature. Because the *Legal News* was the first—and for many years the only—publication which guaranteed almost immediate printing of new laws and court decisions, Illinois lawmakers passed several more acts which recognized the *Legal News* as a certified publisher of legal notices and made the laws and court decisions it published legal evidence in court.

The *Legal News*, with its prompt publication of legal information, became a valuable tool for lawyers. But it was more than a weekly digest of legal mumbo jumbo. Myra reserved space for her sprightly editorials, and they were soon highly popular, especially in the early issues when she focused on topics close to lawyers' hearts—and pocketbooks.

"$750 MADE BY TAKING LEGAL NEWS" crowed one headline. The story that followed told of a Chicago lawyer who, after winning a case in court, asked the judge to rule that the losing party pay his fee. Saying that there was no legal precedent for such a ruling, the judge denied the request. Out the door ran the attorney, rushing back a few minutes later with the latest edition of the *Legal News*, which reported that just three days earlier the legislature had passed an attorneys' fees award act. The judge reversed his decision and ordered the losing side to pay. "You are indebted to Mrs. Bradwell for this!" the judge told the attorney.

Myra also wrote editorials about conditions she felt demeaned the legal profession. She attacked low judicial salaries, pointing out that judges who were not wealthy in

their own right could not "continue on the bench in poverty."
She deplored the conditions of Chicago's Cook County
Courthouse, describing it vividly in her first issue: "The
grass upon the square has been trampled out by boys, cows
and goats. . . . The hall is covered with the accumulated filth
of years, its walls are defaced and decapitated." The courtroom itself was piled with old furniture, she wrote, adding,
". . . if we were the judge instead of the judge's wife we
would order the sheriff to send it to an auction room. . . ."

Myra walked a fine editorial line in her early editorials.
Her understanding of politics told her that to come out too
early and too strong on controversial women's issues would
undermine the support she needed in the legislature. The
prudent way to accomplish this was to remain quiet about
women's issues until the *Legal News* was firmly established. But Myra wasn't interested in playing it safe. From
the first issue, there was no doubt that the *Legal News* would
be an advocate for women, and the surprising events that
occurred during the 1869 Illinois State Constitutional
Convention provided an opportunity for Myra to forcefully
argue her position.

Chapter Four

Bradwell v. Illinois

In February of 1869 the Arctic winds howled across Lake Michigan, rattling windows and slicing through the thin walls of the wood-frame buildings. The snow left the dirt and wooden streets a minefield of holes and ruts and buckled planks. It would seem to be a good time to stay inside, close to the fireplace or coal stove.

Instead, it was a whirlwind season for the Bradwells and their friends, the Waites and Mary Livermore. Beginning that winter they spent the year furiously working to change the laws that kept women in second-class citizenship. Myra also spent some time fighting the battle to be allowed to practice law, a profession she had clearly proven she could master.

The Chicago feminists sent out a call to establish the Illinois Woman Suffrage Association that February, and 3,000 men and women from across the state braved the cold and ice to attend. Myra's work in organizing the meeting was instrumental: she personally persuaded every judge in

Cook County and most leaders of the bar to lend their support.

The meeting was a great success. Mary Livermore was named president, and Myra received high praise from national leaders for her work. Elizabeth Cady Stanton recognized her as "a woman of great force and executive ability."

The association nominated six representatives—the Bradwells, the Waites, Livermore and Stanton—to lobby for women's suffrage at the Constitutional Convention in Springfield. The stakes couldn't have been higher. The Illinois Constitution, last amended in 1848, gave voting rights only to male citizens over the age of twenty-one. If the 1869 convention delegates refused to amend the constitution to allow women the right to vote, no court or legislature could overrule it.

During the convention it became apparent that the delegates would not directly support a women's suffrage amendment. Myra and the other lobbyists looked for a compromise. They asked the convention to submit the women's suffrage amendment to the state's electorate—the eligible male voters—in a referendum. A majority of the convention delegates supported the referendum idea, and it appeared they were ready to vote on it.

But then, in a bitter twist of fate, a stranger from Michigan appeared and single-handedly destroyed the work of several thousand Illinois suffragists. A woman, who called herself

Mrs. Dr. Wheaton of Kalamazoo, in a masterpiece of behind-the-scenes conniving, took over the hall where the convention was meeting. As Susan B. Anthony described it: ". . . afraid that the women of Illinois were about to lose their womanliness by asking for the right to have their opinions counted, . . . [she] gave two lectures against woman suffrage. A meeting was called at the close of the second lecture, and in a resolution moved by a member of the convention . . . without giving a woman of their own State opportunity for reply . . . struck out the clause submitting the question to the people."

Myra summarized the sudden and saddening turn of events eloquently: "The people of the State were told that one woman had proved herself competent and well qualified to enlighten the constitutional convention on the evils of suffrage."

It would have saddened the suffragists even more if they knew then that the stranger from Kalamazoo's success would be the law in Illinois, and in the entire nation, for another fifty years.

All was not lost at the convention, however. Through the efforts of Judges Bradwell and Waite, a constitutional clause was defeated which would have barred Illinois women from either being elected or appointed to public office. It was a small but important victory.

Myra, in the meantime, had a legislative victory of her own. In 1864 the Illinois Supreme Court had ruled that in a marriage, the husband not only had the right to his wife's earnings, he also owned any property the wife brought into the marriage or that she purchased after the wedding. Not content to merely condemn the ruling in *Legal News* editorials, Myra wrote a bill giving married women the right to their earnings and property, took it personally to Springfield, and lobbied it through the General Assembly.

With only the governor's signature now needed for the bill to become law, Myra used her editorials to smooth its passage. She called John Palmer "our noble, honest, and ever watchful governor." Palmer, a family friend, soon signed into law the Married Woman's Property Act.

The Illinois state legislature was becoming a fertile ground for Myra's reform efforts. While she remained supportive of national suffrage work and helped organize the American Woman Suffrage Association in November 1869, she decided to focus her energy closer to home, where she felt it could do the most good.

Although Myra was proving her legal and political expertise every week in the pages of the *Legal News*, as well as in her forays before the legislature, she wanted the prestige that a license to practice law would give. She took the bar exam on August 2, 1869, and passed it with honors.

She was hopeful that the Illinois Supreme Court would accept her petition to be granted a license to practice law. Her friend Sidney Breese was an associate justice, and there were only two other members of the court. (Four justices were added when the new state constitution took effect in 1870.)

In submitting her credentials to the court, Myra wrote an accompanying brief stating, "The only question involved in this case is—Does being a woman disqualify [me] under the law of Illinois from receiving a license to practice law?"

In the winter of 1870 the court decided to not answer Myra's question when it made its decision. Instead, it denied her application, unanimously, on the grounds of the "disability imposed by your married condition."

The "disability" cited was known as "the law of coverture," adapted from British common law, that held that "by marriage the husband and wife are one person in law; that is, the very being or legal existence of the woman is suspended during the marriage, or at least is incorporated . . . into that of the husband; under whose wing, protection, and cover, she performs every thing; . . . her condition during marriage is called coverture . . . And therefore, all deeds executed, and acts done by her, during her coverture are void; . . ."

Of all the reasons the court might have given to reject her application, coverture was surely the last one Myra would have imagined it would use. She had worked as an independent businesswoman for the last year. The Illinois General Assembly had passed a special law enabling her to do exactly what the law of coverture said she couldn't do— own a business separate from her husband. And hadn't the legislature just passed a bill giving married women the right to keep their earnings and their property?

Myra immediately filed a petition asking the court to reconsider its decision. In it she told the court that denying her the right to practice law was "of small consequence" to her personally, but that by using the grounds of women's marital "disability" the justices "strike a blow at the right of every married woman in the great State of Illinois who is dependent on her labor for support, and say to her, you can not enter the smallest contract in relation to your earnings or separate property, that can be enforced against you in a court of law."

The court proved by its next move that it would adroitly do whatever it deemed necessary to keep from granting Myra a license to practice law. The justices praised Myra for "earnestly and ably" arguing against the validity of coverture in her case, adding, "of the qualifications of the applicant we have no doubt." However, the justices unanimously agreed, ". . . we find ourselves constrained to hold that the sex of the applicant, independently of coverture, is, as our law now stands, a sufficient reason for not granting this license."

The Illinois Supreme Court backed its decision with four points. Only the first one pertained even slightly to the laws of Illinois:

First, the court ruled that since the General Assembly had never passed a law allowing women to enter the legal

Chief Justice Salmon P. Chase refused to write a dissenting opinion in the case of *Bradwell v. Illinois*.

profession, it must have intended to bar women from practice.

Second, the justices predicted that admitting a woman to the bar would "open the floodgates," making women eligible for "every civil office" including "governors and sheriffs."

Third, they ruled that the heat of argument in cases before the bar would "tend to destroy the deference and delicacy with which it is a matter of pride of our ruder sex to treat [women]."

Fourth, the justices resorted to long-held predictions that the mere presence of a woman before the bar would prove so distracting to male jurors, attorneys, and judges that the administration of justice itself would be jeopardized.

By the time this decision was handed down, Myra realized that she did not need to be a licensed attorney to achieve her goals. Her hands were more than full with the *Legal News*, her civic and suffrage work, and her family responsibilities. But she wasn't willing to give up the fight. It meant too much to women throughout Illinois, and eventually the entire nation. She found a constitutional attorney to appeal her case to the U.S. Supreme Court.

The case of *Bradwell v. Illinois* dragged on until 1873, when the majority of the U.S. Supreme Court ruled against Myra. Only her relative, Salmon P. Chase, dissented from the majority, but even he refused to write a dissenting opinion. Myra had based her appeal upon the argument that the Constitution protected her right to follow any career legally open to any other citizen, regardless of sex. The court, however, ruled that while all Americans were granted the right to earn a living, that right did not extend to protect any individual's right to pursue a specific profession, such as the law.

The decision was difficult to accept, but Myra refused to grow bitter—or to give up the fight. She returned to the work she did best—whittling away at the laws that handicapped women in their day-to-day lives.

Chapter Five

Great Fire

The battles Myra fought throughout her life did not all take place in a courtroom or in the pages of the *Legal News*. Sometimes she and her family were swept up in events that tragically altered the lives of thousands of other people. One such event was the Chicago Fire.

It seemed as though the summer of 1871 would never end. By the eighth of October, Chicago had endured three months of a drought that scorched the Great Prairie to the west and turned the city's streets to dust.

As darkness fell that Sunday night, Myra and James Bradwell were, like many Chicagoans, worried. A major fire had leveled four square blocks across the river from their home on West Washington Street the night before. On Friday several warehouses had been destroyed by fire.

The Bradwells lived with their two children, fifteen-year old Thomas and Bessie, thirteen, near the heart of Chicago's central business district. They knew that Chicago was more vulnerable to a catastrophic fire than most cities. Their home and offices, and every other structure in the city—factories, hospitals, even the sidewalks and some of the streets—were made of wood. The wrong combination of circumstances could turn Chicago into an inferno.

At 8:45 p.m. their fears were realized. It began with a moment of carelessness in Patrick O'Leary's barn on the southwest side of the city. First, a spark, and soon flames snapped and crackled and exploded into the night sky.

The Chicago Fire Department had lost several pieces of equipment in the earlier fires, and many men and horses had been injured. Those remaining on call had not yet recovered, either physically or mentally.

Next came the terrible mistake: The firefighters were sent to the wrong address. An hour passed before they got to the southwest side of the city, and by then the fire that started in Patrick O'Leary's barn was raging on a course to central Chicago.

Still, it did not seem to be beyond control. The wind was driving the fire north, toward the area that had been consumed in Saturday's fire, and east, toward the broad Chicago River. Both appeared to be natural firebreaks.

But then the law of physics took over. Fed by the heat, the wind picked up, fanning the flames and whipping coals and ash into the air. Wind gusts ripped roofs apart, spewing red-hot shingles from house to house, block to block.

Finally, pockets of super-heated air called "fire devils" began bursting into flame blocks ahead of the fire. As crowds watched from the east bank of the Chicago River, a third of a mile from the blaze, a fire devil shot into their midst, swirling like a tornado. Shouts and screams filled the air as the crowd stampeded to safety. By midnight the fire was raging just four blocks from the heart of the city.

Bells rang and cries of alarm filled the streets as neighbors ran house to house, pounding on doors and windows. Awakened by the noise, the Bradwells ran to their bedroom window. What they saw to the southwest must have looked like the surface of the sun.

They roused their children, packed a few clothes and family heirlooms into a trunk, grabbed the cage holding their pet bird, and ran out the front door. It was pandemonium. The street was jammed with people and wagons, livestock and pets. But at least everyone was headed in the same direction—to the east and the safety of the wide lakefront beaches.

The fire was still several blocks behind the Bradwells as they neared James and Myra's offices. They quickly decided what needed to be saved and where they would meet once they all got to the beach, then Myra and Thomas joined the throng of refugees fleeing to the lakefront.

James and Bessie raced through the offices, picking up a few rare books, photographs of the two Bradwell children who had died in childhood, and the subscription ledger for Myra's weekly newspaper, the *Chicago Legal News.*

James told Bessie to run ahead with the photos and the

A typical scene of the destruction caused by the Chicago Fire of 1871.

ledger. He needed to pick up a few more things and would meet them at the beach as soon as he could.

Out on the street it was total chaos. The smoke was blinding, suffocating. Walls of burning buildings collapsed, blasting flaming timbers in every direction. Confused and afraid, Bessie was swept away in a crowd of frantic people now fleeing to the north side of the city.

When James reached the beach it was literally a sea of humanity. Almost everyone, it seemed, was searching for lost family members. People were pushing in different directions, and it seemed to take forever to worm through the crowds. At last he found Myra and Thomas.

"Where is Bessie?" he asked.

Myra gasped and grabbed his arm: "I thought she was with you."

James was devastated. He had sent Bessie out alone, and now she was lost in the fire.

Taking a deep breath, Myra looked straight into James's eyes and told him, "I'd trust that girl to go to the ends of the earth. She'll come out all right, don't you worry."

James, Myra, and Thomas huddled together, coughing and choking in the smoke, and watched through the night as the inferno turned their home, their city to ash.

The fire was still burning at daybreak, consuming everything as it worked its way north. By Monday evening, when a steady rain mercifully doused its flames, the fire's path of destruction was a mile wide and seven miles long.

The Bradwells, like 90,000 others, lost everything. Still, they believed it was their duty to help with the rescue and salvage efforts. A citizens' meeting was held on Monday night, and James Bradwell got up to speak. He started by telling of the loss of young Bessie.

A man from the crowd interrupted him. "Don't worry, Judge Bradwell," he yelled. "Your daughter is safe on the west side."

Bessie had wandered for nine hours, to the north and then to the south, trying to find a way through the smoldering ruins to the beachfront and her family. At some point she gave the pictures of her dead brother and sister to a family friend for safekeeping; she no longer had the strength to carry them as well as her mother's subscription log. Eventually she trudged across a bridge to the west side where she was found, dazed and exhausted, and taken in by the man who that night shouted to James the miraculous good news.

When Bessie and her family were finally reunited, after all the hugging and kissing and tears of joy, she handed her mother the *Chicago Legal News* ledger. To Myra, it was as if another of her children had been found.

Characteristically, as soon as her family was safely settled, Myra boarded a train for Milwaukee where there were printing facilities available. Three days later that week's edition of the *Chicago Legal News* was printed and ready for distribution—complete and on time.

Chapter Six

A Tall, Bold Slugger

Myra Bradwell and the city of Chicago came of age together, and they shared many characteristics: handsome, vibrant, proud, strong. In his poem "Chicago," Carl Sandburg could have been describing Myra when he called the city ". . . a tall, bold slugger."

Myra's society friends might have blanched at the notion of their charming young colleague as a brawler, but her adversaries would wholeheartedly agree. For as much selfless devotion as she gave to reforming laws for women, as generous and kindhearted as she was in her charitable work, Myra could be a fierce adversary.

She had no qualms about using the *Legal News* as a platform. In the first issue, she lashed out at a Jewish publication that had gently chided her for excluding "a large portion of the bar of the U.S." when she described her paper as a Christian publication. She responded: ". . . we cannot conscientiously add one single plank to accommodate our gallant friends of the Hebrew faith."

She vehemently opposed the practice of paying jurors $1.50 a day for their service. "[This] is an inducement for men having no business of their own and therefore unfit to be trusted with business of other people to foist themselves on the community as jurors."

Judges, legislators, and even her long-time friend, Governor John Palmer, found themselves fiercely attacked in the *Legal News*. When Myra petitioned him to be appointed a notary public, he denied her request based on the law of coverture. Palmer viewed his role and that of the legislature within the strict constitutional limits of the time. He explained this to Myra in a personal note accompanying his decision: "But I will say that while I do not believe you are eligible to the appointment you seek under the law, there is no one I would more cheerfully appoint if the matter were within the limits of my official discretion."

It was a gracious note, but Myra fumed in silence for over two years until, in August of 1872, she printed an anonymous letter from "A Member of the Illinois Legislature": ". . . the legislature was much embarrassed by a crotchety and whimsical governor, . . . he vetoed bills on the most frivolous grounds and was constantly threatening and interfering with members about bills not yet approved by him."

Myra added her commentary to the anonymous letter, noting that she had "the greatest respect" for its author, "one of the ablest members of our General Assembly." Of her friend Governor Palmer, she wrote that "by his peculiar and unreasonable interference, [he had] greatly embarrassed and retarded the action of the legislature."

Nearly twenty years later, in an interview with the *Chicago Tribune*, Myra still couldn't resist taking a verbal swat at Palmer: "However, I have been made an honorary member of the State Bar through the courtesy of ex-Governor Palmer, who, after the denial of my petition to practice law, refused as Governor to grant my petition for appointment as a Notary Public."

Myra's willingness to fight hard to protect her own interests was clearly evident during a typographers' strike in 1874. To put this episode in context of the time, it is important to remember that Chicago was still recovering from the Great Fire of 1871. To make matters worse, there was a nation-wide depression—the Panic of '73. Nearly forty percent of Chicagoans were jobless.

Clearly, this was not the time for unions to strike over frivolous issues. The *Chicago Times* labeled strikers "idiot[s]." A more appropriate term might be desperate. Many workers had been forced to take significant pay cuts; the state's eight-hour work laws were routinely ignored; and ten-year-olds were working the same hours for even less pay.

Myra's commentary in the *Legal News* clearly stated her opinion of the strike. In an article headlined "PAY THEM FOR WORK THEY NEVER DID" she argued the workers

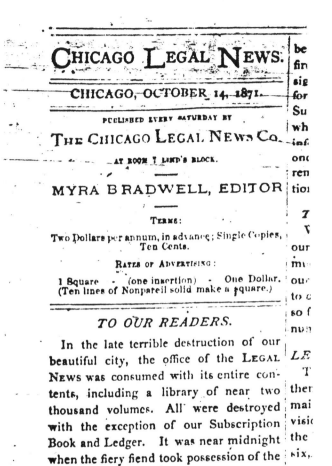

CHICAGO LEGAL NEWS.

CHICAGO, OCTOBER 14, 1871.

PUBLISHED EVERY SATURDAY BY

THE CHICAGO LEGAL NEWS CO.

AT ROOM 7 LIND'S BLOCK.

MYRA BRADWELL, EDITOR

TERMS:

Two Dollars per annum, in advance; Single Copies, Ten Cents.

RATES OF ADVERTISING:

1 Square - (one insertion) - One Dollar. (Ten lines of Nonpareil solid make a square.)

TO OUR READERS.

In the late terrible destruction of our beautiful city, the office of the LEGAL NEWS was consumed with its entire contents, including a library of near two thousand volumes. All were destroyed with the exception of our Subscription Book and Ledger. It was near midnight when the fiery fiend took possession of the block in which we were. Our little daughter Bessie, twelve years of age, rushed into the office, grasped the Subscription Book and the portraits of a brother and sister who are in the spirit world, and went out into the wild night, and, crowd-

This article in the *Chicago Legal News* details the Bradwell family's experience during the 1871 fire.

were asking to be paid for blank pages which separated sections of the legal briefs they printed.

While those pages were obviously not typeset, they still had to be inserted, and the workers felt they should be paid for the work. But Myra disagreed and used the strike to embarrass the union. Myra assailed what she saw as "this unjust and tyrannical demand... TO PAY FOR COMPOSITION ON BLANK PAGES WHICH ARE NEVER SET."

She bragged that although she had been deserted, left with a skeleton staff, she had called in non-union workers "and in three hours after the Union men left our office we were again running. AND OUR PAPER IS OUT IN TIME, FOUR PAGES LARGER THAN ITS USUAL SIZE."

The typographers returned to work in a week, after the union president, as Myra described it, "called at our sanctum and informed us that the Union had rescinded the rule as to blank pages."

Myra had won the battle. She never had union problems again.

Chapter Seven

Figher and Reformer

1872 was an election year and women across the country were attempting to challenge the law's refusal to allow them to vote. In Chicago, Catharine Waite tried to register to vote and was promptly turned away. Susan B. Anthony was a bit more successful in Rochester, New York. Her application to register was accepted, and on Voting Day she marched into the polling place and cast her vote. Shortly thereafter she was indicted, and later tried, by the federal government for "knowingly, wrongfully, and unlawfully" voting in a federal election.

Susan wasted no time in traveling around the country to mobilize suffragists to this latest attack. Myra did her part, using the pages of the *Legal News* to sway opinion to Susan's cause. But a hostile federal judge instructed the jury to convict, which it did. The judge had the authority to send Susan to prison but restrained himself (probably in light of the outrage her imprisonment would cause) and instead fined her $100, which she refused to pay.

One success of 1872 was the election of James Bradwell to a seat in the Illinois General Assembly. James quickly earned a reputation as an aggressive, and successful, advocate for women's rights. Before he even took his seat, James was instrumental in getting the legislature to pass a bill prohibiting discrimination against women in any occupation other than the military. The law was routinely ignored, even by the courts, but at least it was on the books.

Myra helped with James's legislative work. She often wrote the bills that he sponsored in the General Assembly, including one that made all women—married as well as single—eligible for appointment as a notary public.

They also got the legislature to enact a bill giving women the right to run for office in Illinois school board elections. The irony of women running for offices they weren't allowed to vote for was not wasted on Myra. "If women hold office, why should they not be allowed to vote? . . . We predict that this is the first in a series of acts which will aid in extending the right of suffrage in Illinois," she wrote.

Myra's prediction was correct, but her schedule was optimistic. She didn't live to see women given the right to vote in most elections. However, she did live to see Illinois women granted the right to vote in school elections in 1891.

Most of the reforms Myra and James advocated became law or policy during the 1870s. They helped remove some of the corruption from the Chicago courthouse and the entire Illinois judicial system. With James using his considerable power of verbal persuasion and Myra her writing skills in the *Legal News*, they had liquor removed from the courtrooms as well as the jury rooms; they put an end to attorneys bribing jurors or packing juries with their friends; and they forced judges and attorneys to demonstrate, through their behavior in the courtroom, proper respect for the legal system they were sworn to uphold.

Myra also insisted that prospective lawyers have a solid understanding of the law before taking the bar exam. She published guidebooks which included extensive reading lists. She was among the first to call for a professional association of attorneys—a bar association—with strict standards of knowledge and accomplishment for membership. The Chicago and Illinois bar associations formed in part due to Myra's advocacy, and she was made an honorary member of the state association upon nomination of none other than her favorite scoundrel, Governor John Palmer.

It would be a great mistake to assume that Myra skipped from success to success during these years. She may not have been subject to constant anti-feminist hostility which haunted radicals like Susan B. Anthony, but she suffered the usual scorn and ridicule directed toward feminists. She was labeled a homewrecker, an Amazon man-hater, or a swishy-skirted twit whose flirtations could addle men's brains and destroy their will. Myra came in for particularly nasty attention in 1873 when she went to hear the case of *Bradwell v. Illinois*. One corespondent reported that: "Her personal manners [were] outrageously aped; her speech falsely reported—while the idle curious followed her about the streets of Washington as if she were some animal from the jungle!"

The editors of *The Nation* used the occasion of her Supreme Court appearance to cry out against the "ludicrous illustration" of "the effect produced by legal study on the female mind." Here was this "prominent female agitator," the editors crowed, who was trying to "prove the fitness of her sex for professional life by taking for her first important case one which she must have known the court would decide against her, unless she either supposed that they were likely to be influenced by personal solicitation and clamor, or else they were all gone crazy."

The Nation's editors thought that Myra's study of the law had damaged her fragile female brain to the point that she imagined she could make a losing case a winner before the Supreme Court.

Myra found the public humiliation hard to take, as have other social reformers, before and since. She well-knew that some public crusaders choose to quit rather than subject themselves and their families to the continued harassment. Catharine Waite, for example, after touring the state as president of the Illinois Woman Suffrage Association in 1871 and calling for "a society for woman suffrage in every county and town in the State," withdrew from public life.

But Myra seemed to grow strong on a diet of adversity.

Myra corresponded with Susan B. Anthony during her struggle to be
admitted to the Illinois Bar Association.

She could always rip an adversary to shreds with her pen. But she was equally adept at using humor to score a point, and it may well be that her sense of humor is what carried her through the most bitter of times. To illustrate an editorial criticizing the courtroom behavior of certain judges, she offered this: "A certain pompous judge fined several lawyers $10 each for contempt of court. After they had paid their fines, a steady-going old attorney walked gravely up to the bench and laid down a $10 bill. 'What is this for?' inquired the judge.

'For contempt, your honor.'

'Why, I have not fined you for contempt.'

'I know that,' said the attorney, 'but I want you to understand that I cherish a secret contempt for this court all the time, and I'm willing to pay for it.'"

Even the most humorless of her readers must have let out a guffaw after reading her story about a bar applicant in neighboring Indiana:

"What's the first duty of an attorney?" asked the presiding judge. To which the young attorney responded, "To secure his fees, sir."

Peels of laughter racked the courtroom. Once everything was back under control, the judge turned to the clerk and said, "Prepare a license for this applicant. I find him well qualified to practice law in the state of Indiana."

As an editor, Myra had little tolerance for either lawyers or expert witnesses who baffled jurors with highly technical language. "Scientific evidence," she wrote, "should be as unscientific as possible. I wonder what [a doctor] called a bruise before 'ecchymosis' was naturalized?"

Myra's writing talent was a pleasure to the lawyers who read her newspaper. She infused the dry format of legal publishing with a readable and entertaining style, providing accurate news with a format they enjoyed. That combination gave her a powerful leverage to directly influence courtrooms and legislatures throughout the country.

Chapter Eight

Reason Restored

During the 1800s Illinois law described the mentally ill as "idiots, lunatics and distracted persons." Illinois law further established standards under which people (the physically and mentally handicapped were often included) could be committed to an institution against their will. Property owners had the right to a jury trial to determine whether they were or were not insane. If they were found insane, the judge was required to appoint a conservator to oversee the person's interests for as long as they were confined.

People who did not own property could be committed at any time on the word of a relative, acquaintance, or a magistrate. Prior to the establishment of the State Hospital for the Insane in 1851, the poor could either be sent to a poorhouse or a prison.

The name of the institution mattered little, though. For once a person was committed, release back into society was highly unlikely. People who were sane at the time of their commitment often slipped into madness after a few months in a dungeon-like, scream-filled asylum.

For those who could not own property—women and children—the husband or father could commit them on his word alone.

In his law practice, James Bradwell saw horrible abuses of the commitment laws. A man could drag his wife to an asylum for simply disagreeing with him; he could dump one or all of his children into a state run hospital—forever. This was one of the reasons James and Myra worked so hard to get the Married Woman's Property Act passed in the 1869 General Assembly.

A former asylum inmate, Elizabeth Packard, was one of the Bradwells' closest allies in this fight. Like Myra, Elizabeth was a free spirit. At the time of her commitment, in 1860, she was forty-four years old and the mother of six children. Her husband, Theophilus, was a minister, fifteen years older than Elizabeth. She had grown to view his religious beliefs as "stodgy."

Elizabeth experimented with what today would be called New Age ideas. She tried phrenology (using the shape of the skull to analyze a person's character and destiny), and later became a believer in a form of spiritualism called Swedenborgianism, after an eighteenth century philosopher and mystic.

Her escapades into the religious fringe might have been passed off as merely unorthodox had she not been married to a minister. For Elizabeth to step outside her accepted wifely role was an intolerable embarrassment for Theophilus. He called her mad. But it wasn't until she decided to join another faith—the Methodist—that the Reverend called in the sheriff. He also brought in two doctors from his congregation who took Elizabeth's pulse and pronounced her insane.

Elizabeth spent three long years in the state insane asylum. There she found a number of other women who, like herself, had been committed because of their religious beliefs. Any or all of them could have been released if they had renounced their beliefs and promised to return to their husbands' sides.

Elizabeth not only refused to back down on her beliefs, she launched into verbal battle with the asylum's superintendent. She was smart and articulate, and her obvious mental competence (perhaps even superiority) eventually convinced the superintendent to release Elizabeth into her husband's custody in June, 1863.

After her release, Elizabeth went before the court to clear her name, and in early 1864 she was declared sane. She then began a personal crusade to reform the nation's mental commitment laws.

In 1867, Elizabeth stood alone before the Illinois General Assembly and told the story of her commitment, of the horrible conditions inside the state asylum, and of her lengthy fight. She stunned the lawmakers into action. Within a few months they unanimously passed a bill requiring a jury trial before anyone could be committed to an insane asylum.

The law was far from ideal—trial by jury was a horrible ordeal for the mentally ill—but it gave women, children, and the poor more protection than they had ever had before.

Little did the Bradwells know that in a few years they would have to find ways around that law to fight for the freedom of another mental patient: the martyred president's widow, Mary Todd Lincoln.

Even before her husband's assassination, Mary Todd Lincoln suffered from long bouts of depression, often accompanied by violent headaches that became worse after a near-fatal head injury that resulted from a carriage wreck in 1863. But the "craziness" that Mary became notorious for, and that most caught the attention of Robert, her only surviving son, was her obsession for buying clothes. She often spent hundreds of dollars a week, sometimes in a single day, on dresses, shoes, gloves, and jewelry.

Mary's buying compulsion worsened after the president's death, and worse yet after the death of her son Tad in 1871. She hoarded her purchases, filling dozens of trunks with clothes she never wore. In addition to the compulsive shopping, she became paranoid that people were trying to steal her money. When she returned to Chicago in 1875—drawn there because she imagined that Robert was deathly ill—she carried her entire fortune in cash and bonds sewn into her petticoats.

Mary had constant stomach pains that her doctors could not explain. She became convinced someone was poisoning her; more often she thought the pains were caused by the chloral hydrate she took constantly to calm her nerves and help her sleep. Today we know that chloral hydrate damages the liver and kidneys and can cause hallucinations. We also know it is highly addictive. But in the 1870s it was believed to be a perfectly harmless drug.

After Mary returned to Chicago, Robert Lincoln became more aware of his mother's problems. He was also concerned that she would deplete all the family money. He decided to have her committed to an asylum.

The debate still continues over Robert's motivation for having Mary committed. Some argue he was overwhelmingly motivated by his wish to seize control of any money his mother had not yet spent. Others point out that because of the laws James Bradwell had pushed through the Illinois legislature Mary's money and property were protected from seizure; therefore Robert had Mary's well-being foremost in mind. Whatever was his motivation, Robert probably had little reason to suspect that his action would result in such unwanted and embarrassing publicity.

On May 19, 1875, the president's widow had finished her noon meal and was resting in her room at Chicago's elegant Grand Union Hotel. She had been living in the hotel, under guard, for two months. Mary had probably taken a dose of chloral after her lunch; it was less likely to upset

Mary Todd Lincoln suffered emotional problems in the years after President Lincoln's assassination.

her stomach after a meal. So when Robert's attorney, Leonard Swett, appeared at her hotel room and told her he was taking her to court for a sanity hearing, she was well sedated. To all the observers who saw her in the crowded courtroom, Mary appeared, dressed in her customary widow's clothes, to be calm, even disinterested.

Despite all the protection available to Mary under the law, her trial has been called a "kangaroo court"—a mockery of justice, with every shred of evidence stacked against her. Robert Lincoln and Leonard Swett had arranged for all the witnesses to testify for commitment, failed to give her notice of the proceedings so that she could arrange for legal counsel, and had even hired the attorney who represented Mary in court.

Mary's lawyer, Isaac Arnold, believed she was insane. As the trial began, he took Robert's attorney aside to tell him that he could not fairly defend her. "That means that you will put into her head," Leonard shouted, "that she can get some mischievous lawyer to make us trouble; go and defend her and do your duty."

Not surprisingly, Mary was found insane and committed to an asylum.

After the verdict was read, Robert came to Mary's side. He had been crying. "It's for the best, Mother."

At last Mary spoke, without emotion: "Oh, Robert, to think that my son would ever have done this."

Mary returned to the Grand Union Hotel, but that night

she slipped past her hotel-room guards and attempted to buy a lethal dose of laudanum—a mixture of opium and alcohol which, like chloral, could then be bought without prescription. The druggists in the area had been warned about Mary and two refused to sell it to her. The third told her to come back in one-half hour and sent for Robert. When Robert did not appear, the druggist mixed some burnt-sugar and water and sold it to Mary as laudanum.

Robert still had not shown up when Mary returned a third time, saying the "medicine" hadn't worked. The druggist, frantic by this time, stalled again, then mixed another harmless concoction, labeled it "Laudanum—Poison" and gave it to her.

Robert arrived shortly thereafter. The next day, he and Leonard Swett took her to Bellevue Place, a private sanitarium in Batavia, forty miles west of Chicago.

The news of Mary's insanity trial stunned the nation. She hadn't been a popular First Lady, but many people were outraged by the way Robert treated her. Among the outraged were Myra and James Bradwell. They knew Mary well. She had bought a house near theirs on West Washington Street shortly after the president's death. In the year Mary lived there, the Bradwells befriended her. James had even handled her will.

As unjust as they felt Mary's trial had been, the Bradwells weren't sure whether they could, or should, intervene. They knew that she was troubled. Perhaps the privacy of Bellevue, the quietness of the countryside, was what Mary wanted for herself—to get out of the public eye, to relax, to heal.

Mary's living conditions at Bellevue were superior to a state institution. Bellevue was small—only twenty patients during Mary's stay—and admitted "only a select class of lady patients," who were "only moderately troubled." Mary had a private room, away from other patients in the doctor's house, and she was free to walk the grounds or take carriage rides at any time.

Although drugs like chloral hydrate, morphine, marijuana, and even beer and wine were routinely used to calm Bellevue patients, Mary's access to drugs was strictly limited. Her physical and mental improvement were rapid.

In the meantime, Mary was plotting. As relatively pleasant as her situation was, she was still a prisoner. She particularly hated the bars on the windows and the fact that she was not allowed to send or receive letters without Robert's permission.

Robert visited weekly, and throughout Mary's first two months at Bellevue he maintained the mail ban. Finally, in late July, he gave her permission to write to her older sister, Elizabeth Todd Edwards, in Springfield. Mary felt that if she could get Elizabeth to agree to take her in, Robert could be persuaded to release her from Bellevue.

But Mary was also savvy enough to realize that, in addition to Elizabeth, she needed some strong political muscle to back her. That afternoon she smuggled four more letters to be posted with her sister's—one of them addressed to Myra and James Bradwell, begging for their help.

As soon as they read the letter, the Bradwells began plotting as well. They chose to skirt the legal system, relying instead on Myra's most fearsome weapon—publicity. She would not only use it to convince the public that Mary deserved her freedom, she would use it to personally attack Robert and Bellevue's director, Dr. Richard Patterson, as unjust and inhumane captors.

Once her strategy was in place, Myra traveled to Bellevue, marched straight to the doctor's house and rang the bell. The doctor himself answered, and after much discussion told Myra that he would not allow either letters or visitors without Robert's written approval.

"If she is only permitted to see such persons as you choose," Myra argued, "and is not permitted to receive letters except from such, *she is virtually a prisoner, is she not?*"

"Madame," the doctor replied, "she is no more so than other patients I have under my care."

With that, Myra pretended to back down. Then she asked if she might wait in the parlor until it was time for her train back to Chicago. The doctor agreed and then left her alone.

Imagine his horror at seeing the headline a few days later:

MRS. LINCOLN

Is the Widow of President Lincoln a Prisoner?

No One Allowed to See Her Except by Order of Her Son

An Account of a Remarkable Interview With Her Jailer and Physician

In the article that followed, Myra went on to describe her trip to Batavia, her confrontation with Dr. Patterson, and her stay in the parlor: "It struck me as being rather strange [not seeing any patients around], inasmuch as I had heard his patients had the freedom of the house, but this, clearly, must be an erroneous impression of a good-natured public."

The doctor, in other words, had made fools of the trusting citizens. And Myra knew that they, in turn, would view Dr. Patterson as the villain in this story.

She then described how she would feel, deserted by her friends and family, with little hope for release: "It would take but a few days to make a raving maniac of me." She did her literary best to wrench her readers' hearts: "Surrounded by those whose reason is dethroned, kept a prisoner to all intents and purposes, having no voice as to who shall see me or call on me . . . knowing that I was constantly watched and every move known; soon, very soon, would all interest in life cease, and if death did not end the darkness that moved over me, the seal of insanity would surely be written upon my brain, and all that remained of life would go out in that hour."

Finally, she jolted her readers back to the point: "Mrs. Lincoln recently said she would gladly surrender her bonds for her liberty, as money would not replace that nor give back to her the affection of those for whom she would be glad to live and for whom she would lay down her life."

Without mentioning Robert's name, Myra put him squarely in the villain's seat with Dr. Patterson. What kind of son could betray his dear mother, who only loved him, forgave him, and remained loyal to him in return?

Mary Lincoln may have been crazy, but no one could call her stupid. She had found in Myra a she-bear who would fight without mercy on her behalf.

Robert backed down quickly. Myra visited Mary frequently over the next few weeks, and they wrote almost daily. James and Myra also wrote to Elizabeth Todd Edwards, trying to convince her that Mary was well enough to complete her recovery at the Edwards' home.

August 7, a Saturday, was the start of Phase Two of Myra's publicity campaign. It was common knowledge that the doctor spent his Saturdays away from Bellevue. With his permission, Myra visited Mary on Friday and stayed the night with her.

Myra briefly left Bellevue on Saturday morning. When she returned, she was accompanied by a man who signed the guest ledger as "Mr. Wilkie of Chicago." Mary knew Franc B. Wilkie from her White House days, when he was a *New York Times* reporter. His visit on that day was as a reporter for the *Chicago Times.*

Over the next two hours, Myra sat quietly nearby as Franc interviewed Mary in her room. Whether Myra told him before the interview what questions he could and could not ask, we do not know. But we can be almost certain that on Friday night the two women thoroughly rehearsed the way in which Mary would present herself—calm, reasoned, sane. It worked. When Franc Wilkie left, he was convinced of Mary's sanity. He returned to Chicago to write his article. But he would not publish it immediately.

By this time, Elizabeth Todd Edwards had been persuaded that Mary was at least well enough to come for an extended visit. Although they still believed Mary was better off confined to Bellevue, Richard Patterson's and Robert's defenses were wearing down. Perhaps it would be best for all concerned if Mary spent some time under her sister's supervision in Springfield.

That was before they learned of the unauthorized visit by "Mr. Wilkie of Chicago." Richard and Robert were furious, even though they didn't know at the time that Wilkie was a reporter. Elizabeth was taken aback, as well, not by Wilkie but by Myra and Mary's misinterpretation of her invitation for Mary's "visit." To Elizabeth it meant a few days at most; to Myra and Mary it meant permanent release.

Myra must have known that Wilkie's visit would create a furor. Perhaps she thought Mary's captors would cave in to the pressure. But she underestimated her adversaries and she overestimated Mary's ability to deal with the renewed conflict.

Elizabeth withdrew her invitation, telling Robert she was not willing to "assume any responsibility." Further, she explained that due to her own health problems she was "a most unfit person to control an unsound mind."

Richard and Robert both wrote to Myra, warning her to restrict her own visits and to never again bring an unauthorized person to Bellevue Place. Robert also told her that Elizabeth was no longer able to take Mary in. Then he pulled the trump card: Mary's old symptoms had returned. He blamed this on "the constant excitement she has been in since your last visit."

Believing that this had settled the question of Mary's release for the time being, Robert then left on vacation. Myra couldn't have planned it better herself.

On August 24, the *Chicago Times* headline blared:

REASON RESTORED

Mrs. Lincoln Will Soon Return from Her Brief Visit to the Insane Asylum.

For Her Physicians Pronounce Her as Sane as Those Who Sent Her There.

And She is Only Awaiting Robert's Return from the

East to Set Her Free Again.

How She Talked with a "Times" Correspondent
in a Recent Interview.

Her Recollection of Past Events and What She
had to Say of Them.

What Mrs. Myra Bradwell Has Been Doing in Her
Behalf.

The article that followed was only a little more detailed than the lengthy headline, with one exception, of course. Those "Physicians" who "Pronounced Her . . . Sane" were not interviewed. Instead, Wilkie quoted Myra as saying that Dr. Patterson signed a "certificate of [Mrs. Lincoln's] recovery" and that Robert agreed to Mary's release to live with Elizabeth.

Whether or not the reporter knew that these statements were false, Myra certainly did. For only a few days earlier, James had written a letter to Dr. Patterson in which he threatened to take legal action if Mary were not released to Elizabeth's care.

But journalistic standards were not what they are today. So rather than verifying Myra's statements with the doctor, Franc presented himself as a medical watchdog—"a Representative of THE TIMES, in quest of scientific facts by means of personal observation"—and thus determined that

Robert Lincoln made the mistake of underestimating Myra Bradwell.

"No mental weakness, under any possible test, could be discovered."

He concluded dramatically, saying ". . . whatever condition of mind Mrs. Lincoln may have been in previously, she is unquestionably *compos mentis* now, and ought not to be deprived of her liberty."

The walls surrounding Mary were crumbling in earnest now. Richard Patterson tried to defend himself in a letter which the *Times* published on August 28:

". . . I have not at any time regarded [Mary] as a person of sound mind.. . . I believe her to be now insane. . . ."

Her release, he wrote, ". . . will result only in giving her the coveted opportunity to make extended rambles, to renew the indulgence of her purchasing mania, and other morbid fascinations."

James counter-attacked in an interview with the *Chicago Post and Mail.* As printed in the article, he said he had found "NOT THE SLIGHTEST TRACE OF INSANITY" in his dealings with Mary. He then said, "DR. PATTERSON IS A VERY PECULIAR MAN" whose motives he did not trust. "But, if she is not soon out," James warned, "there will be startling developments not to be mentioned now."

By the time Robert learned of the situation public sympathy had rallied to Mary's side. Feeling the pressure, Elizabeth changed her mind again, and on September 10 Robert escorted his mother to Elizabeth's home in Springfield.

Richard Patterson's predictions soon proved to be true. When Mary left Elizabeth's to live in France, nine months after her release from Bellevue Place, the floors in her room were sagging from the weight of her purchases in Springfield.

Mary's years in France were characterized not only by her continued "purchasing mania" but by what she called her "Great Bloat"—a massive weight gain. By 1880 she was desperately ill. Her weight dropped to one hundred pounds, and she was so weak she had trouble walking.

Mary eventually returned to Elizabeth's, where she stayed in her room with the shades drawn. She wore a money belt day and night. She heard Lincoln's voice and slept on only one side of the bed to keep "the President's place." When she got out of bed, it was only to open her trunks—there were now sixty-four of them—and fondle her possessions.

Elizabeth cared for her sister until Mary's death in July, 1882. It is not known if the Bradwells had any personal contact with Mary after her release from Bellevue Place.

Chapter Nine

Last Years

By the mid-1870s, the *Chicago Legal News* had earned a national reputation. Its readership ranged from backwoods lawyers to Supreme Court justices, and through its pages they witnessed a revolution in their profession.

The Chicago Legal News Company was now a publishing empire that brought in a small fortune to the Bradwells. They had a comfortable home on posh Michigan Avenue. They sent both Bessie and Thomas to law school. Bessie graduated first in her class at what would later become Northwestern University.

Much of the corporate profit went back into her publishing business, of course. Among her newer employees were associate editors and assistant managers who took over some of her more burdensome work. But there was always one job that Myra insisted on doing herself. After each session of the General Assembly, Myra took her proof copy of that session's *Revised Statutes of the State of Illinois* to Springfield and personally double-checked every word against the originals before printing the final documents.

James left the state legislature at the end of his second term, in 1877. In addition to resuming his law practice, he began work on the first of twenty volumes entitled *Reports of the Decisions of the Appellate Court of the State of Illinois: 1877-1887*, which Myra published annually.

Well into his fifties in the 1880s, James was an imposing figure on the streets and in the courtrooms of Chicago. He was considered a legal expert by then, one of the stalwarts of his profession. His height and his muscular physique were now dramatically accented by a mane of white hair and a neatly trimmed beard.

With her expanded staff, Myra now had the freedom to take time off. Always the hometown cheerleader, one of her early leaves took her to Philadelphia to promote Chicago's contribution in the 1876 World's Exposition. She and James took several trips to Europe, as well—just for fun.

As they grew older, Myra and James devoted less time to the cases that had so consumed their earlier years. Myra became a mentor and advocate for several young women who were attempting to break through the remaining barriers to female lawyers, and was more than willing to roar back into her old style if she thought it necessary to right a wrong. Belva Lockwood of Washington, D.C., and Lavinia Goodell, who lived in Wisconsin, were two of Myra's proteges in the legal profession.

A law school graduate who had been admitted to the

District of Columbia bar, Belva Lockwood was not allowed to take a client's case into federal court. The chief justice simply told her, by way of explanation: "Mistress Lockwood, you are a woman."

When Myra Bradwell heard of these words, she began a campaign much like the one she had waged on her own behalf years before. In the *Legal News* she began hammering away at Belva's adversaries. Often she quoted directly from the transcripts of Belva's court hearings, using the federal judges' own words to make fools of them.

Myra also relied on her lobbying skills. The fight to gain women lawyers access to the federal bar took five years, but finally a woman's right to plead cases in federal court was opened to women by an act of Congress. Many state courts, however, continued to bar women attorneys, including Belva's neighboring state of Maryland, which she was dismayed to discover when she attempted to try a case there.

Throughout Belva's ordeal, Myra was also doing battle on behalf of Lavinia Goodell. Lavinia's was an especially rambunctious crusade for Myra, due to the archaic notions of Wisconsin's Chief Justice Ryan.

In his first ruling denying Lavinia's right to practice law, Justice Ryan expounded on women's destiny under the "law of nature" to be wives, mothers and homemakers. Forsaking her "sacred duties" to become a lawyer was, in Justice Ryan's mind, a departure "from the order of nature; and, when voluntary, treason against it."

In his later years, James Bradwell was an imposing figure in the courtrooms of Chicago.

Ryan could not have better chosen words certain to engage Myra's full attention. Myra took after him mercilessly in her editorials. Even after Lavinia's battle was won, and she was no longer denied the right to follow her chosen profession, Myra took every opportunity to criticize and humiliate Justice Ryan. Her tendency to turn political fights into personal vendettas may not have been one of Myra's more admirable characteristics, but it certainly put potential adversaries on notice that she had to be taken seriously.

But Myra also used the *Legal News* to celebrate women's victories outside the legal world. When *Harper's Bazaar* offered its editor, Mary L. Booth, the unheard-of salary of $8000, Myra announced it proudly to her readers. And you could almost hear her cheering when she reported that the Secretary of the U.S. Treasury had made a woman the captain of a Mississippi steamboat.

A new challenge appealed to Myra as the 400th anniversary of Columbus' discovery of America neared. The World's Columbian Exposition was planned to celebrate the event, and competition between the major cities such as New York, Philadelphia, Boston, St. Louis, and Chicago, was intense. Myra led the campaign organized to bring the spectacle to her home town. After middle-aged Myra and her delegation of Chicagoans descended on Washington to argue their case, it quickly became obvious the other cities didn't have a chance. Chicago got the nod. Myra and crew went home and began turning Jackson Park, a respectable-

The Ferris Wheel first made its appearance at the 1893 World's Columbian Exposition held in Chicago's Jackson Park.

sounding name for a 633-acre lakeside marsh, into the home of the World's Columbian Exposition.

In three frantic years, Myra and her crew transformed the swamp into a wonderland with wide boardwalks winding past fountains and pools to a classical "White City" that featured seventeen major exhibit buildings and dozens of smaller ones. It took seven thousand workers and ten million dollars to complete, but the World's Columbian Exposition of 1893 (one year late—as Myra would say, *the impossible just takes a little longer*) is still remembered as one of the greatest world fairs.

Myra had the honor of being appointed one of the exhibition's "Lady Managers." Of course, for Myra, this was a working appointment. She threw her energies into overall planning, recruiting, organizing and promoting. As if that weren't enough, Myra was chair of the Auxiliary Congress's Committee on Law Reform.

But something was wrong. Myra had always retained the sturdy figure of her girlhood, as well as her dark curls and pink cheeks. She now began to tire easily. Her rosy complexion turned ghostly. She was eating like a bird, and her clothes began to hang on her once pleasantly plump body. She was not surprised when her doctors revealed that she had cancer.

Did she retreat to her mansion to die? Of course not. This was Myra Colby Bradwell, the woman who never met a fight she didn't relish. She knew there was no winning this

Upon her death in 1894 the *American Bar Review* called Myra Bradwell "one of the most remarkable women of her generation."

one in an era when there was no treatment for cancer, but she wasn't going to sit around and wait to die.

If the Columbian Exposition—the *Chicago World's Exposition*—was to be Myra's last hurrah, she was determined it would go up with a bang. And she was not about to give up on her *Legal News*, either. She worked as she had always done. She rested when she could go no longer, and then got up to work until the weakness knocked her down again.

Eventually, 27.5 million people attended the six-month fair. On opening day, Myra visited the exhibits in her wheelchair. Over the next weeks, she and James returned again and again, to see the sights, to address conferences, to charm the world's elite at society functions, but most importantly to cherish these last days in *their* magnificent city by the lake.

During the months of Myra's illness, James did something he had never done before—he took on a project that he kept secret from her. He began a letter writing campaign and sent pleas to the high courts of Springfield, Illinois and Washington, D.C. In April 1890, Myra received a notice from the Illinois Supreme Court that she proudly printed in the *Chicago Legal News*: "We are pleased to say that last week, upon the original record, every member of the Supreme Court of Illinois, cordially acquiesced in granting, on the court's own motion, a license as an attorney and counselor at law to Mrs. Bradwell."

Two years later, in 1892, Myra received a similar notice from the U.S. Supreme Court. In both cases the decisions were made retroactive until 1869, the date of her original application for admission to the bar. This officially made Myra Bradwell America's first woman lawyer.

Myra died at home on February 14, 1894, two days after her sixty-third birthday. Her obituaries were eloquent.

"One of the most remarkable women of her generation."—*American Bar Review.*

"No more powerful and convincing argument in favor of the admission of women to a participation in the administration of government was ever made, than can be found in her character, conduct and achievements."—*Illinois State Bar Association.*

But perhaps the most poignant, the one feminists may hate but which says it all in a most nineteenth century way, comes from *A Woman of the Century*:

"Notwithstanding her profession and her numerous activities, [Myra Bradwell] is a favorite in the society of Chicago."

Few women of any day could so successfully influence such starkly contrasting worlds—radical reform and the conservative elite. That Myra did it, with flair and good cheer, is testimony to her faith in herself, in the basic goodness of others, and in the power of free voices to change the course of a nation.

Timeline

1831 Born Myra Colby, February 12, 1831, in Manchester, VT.

1837 Abolitionist Elijah Lovejoy murdered by pro-slavery mob.

1843 Colby family moves to Elgin, IL.

1852 Myra elopes with James Bradwell; they move to Memphis, TN. First child, Myra, born 1853, dies 1861.

1854 Bradwells move to Chicago; James starts law practice with Myra's brother Frank. Three children born in Chicago: Thomas, 1856; Bessie, 1858; James, 1862, dies 1864.

1860-65 Myra works on the home front during the Civil War.

1868 First edition of *Chicago Legal News*, Oct. 3.

1869 Myra passes Illinois State Bar exam with honors; denied admission to practice law by the Illinois Supreme Court on the grounds she was a woman. Organizes first woman's suffrage association in Illinois in February; helps organize American Woman's Suffrage Association in November.

1871 The Chicago fire destroys an area seven miles long and one mile wide; the Bradwells' home and both businesses are lost.

1872 Myra is made an honorary member of the Illinois Bar Association. James is elected to the first of two terms in the state House of Representatives, becomes known for his "zealous" advocacy of reforms for women.

1875 Myra and James campaign for Mary Todd Lincoln's release from an insane asylum.

1890 Illinois Supreme Court admits Myra to practice law; Myra lobbies Congress to make Chicago the site of Columbian World's Exposition.

1892 Myra admitted to practice before the U.S. Supreme Court.

1894 Myra dies of cancer, February 14.

Sources

Chapter One—Abolitionist Childhood

p.12   "ladies and gentlemen of color . . ." Edward Magdol, *Owen Lovejoy: Abolitionist in Congress* (Rutgers University Press, New Brunswick, NJ, 1967) 41.

Chapter Two—Civil War Years

p.16   "the acknowledged belle of Elgin" Jane M. Friedman, *America's First Woman Lawyer* (Prometheus Books, Buffalo, NY, 1993) 87.

p.20   "natural gifts as an eloquent . . ." *Dictionary of American Biography, Vol. 2.* (Charles Scribners Sons, New York, 1966) 580.

p.22   "Do not let any power . . ." Magdol, 360.

p.23   "Mrs. Judge Bradwell devoted . . ." Friedman, 42.

Chapter Three—Chicago Legal News

p.24   "I believe that married people . . ." Friedman, 38-39.

p.30   "the most important legal publication . . ." *Notable American Women, 1607-1950: A Biographical Dictionary, Vol. 1.* (Belknap Press of Harvard University Press, 1971) 225.

p.31   "$750 MADE BY TAKING . . ." Friedman, 79

p.32   "continue on the bench in poverty." Friedman, 114.

p.32   "The grass upon the square . . ." Friedman, 114.

Chapter Four—Bradwell v. Illinois

p.35   ". . . afraid that the women . . ." Friedman, 175.

p.35   "The people of the State . . ." Friedman, 175.

p.36   "Our noble, honest, and watchful governor." Friedman, 201.

p.37   "The only question involved in this case . . ." Friedman 18.

p.37   "disability imposed by your married condition" Friedman, 20.

p.37   "by marriage the husband and wife . . ." Friedman, 19.

p.38   "of small consequence . . ." Friedman, 20.

p.38   "earnestly and ably . . ." Friedman, 20.

p.40   "open the floodgates . . ." Friedman, 20.

Chapter Five—Great Fire

p.46   "Where is Bessie . . ." Friedman, 87.

p.47   "Don't worry, Judge Bradwell . . ." Friedman, 88.

Chapter Six—A Tall, Bold Slugger

p.48   ". . . a tall bold slugger . . ." Carl Sandburg, *Illinois Poets: A Selection* (University of Illinois Press, Carbondale, IL, 1968), 38.

p.48   "a large portion of the bar of the U.S." Friedman, 102.

p.48   ". . . we cannot conscientiously . . ." Friedman, 103.

p.49   "[This] is an inducement . . ." Friedman, 107.

p.49   "But I will say . . ." Friedman, 164.

p.49   ". . . the legislature was much embarrassed . . ." Friedman, 156-157.

p.49   "the greatest respect . . ." Friedman, 157.

p.50   "idot[s]." John H. Keiser, *Building for the Centuries: Illinois, 1865-1898* (The University of Illinois Press, Urbana, IL, 1977), 262.

p.50   "PAY THEM FOR WORK . . ." Friedman, 85.

Chapter Seven—Fighter and Reformer

p.53   "knowingly, wrongfully, and unlawfully" Friedman, 182-183.

p.54   "If women held office . . ." *Chicago Legal News* (*CLN*), April 5, 1873, 330.

p.55   "Her personal manners . . ." Eleanor Gridley, "Presentation of Bronze Bust of Mrs. Myra Bradwell, First Woman Lawyer of Illinois." (*Transactions of the Illinois Historical Society, No. 38*, 1931), 24.

p.56   "ludicrous illustration . . ." "The Supreme Court Righting Itself" (*The Nation, No. 16*, April 24, 1873), 280.

p.56   "a society for woman suffrage . . ." *Notable American Women*, 524.

p.58   "A certain pompous judge . . ." *CLN*, July 15, 1876, 341.

p.58   "What's the first duty . . ." Herman Kogan, *The First Century: The Chicago Bar Association, 1874-1974* (Rand McNally & Co., Chicago, 1974), 30.

p.59   "Scientific evidence . . ." *CLN*, May 21, 1887, 297

Chapter Eight—Reason Restored

p.60   "idiots, lunatics and distracted persons." Mark E. Neely Jr. and R. Gerald McMurtry, *The Insanity File: The Case of Mary Todd Lincoln* (Southern Illinois University Press, Carbondale, IL, 1986), 18-19.

p.61   "stodgy." Neely and McMurtry, 19.

p.66   "That means that you will put into her head. . ." Neely and McMurtry, 58.

p.66   "It's for the best, mother . . ." David R. Collins, *Shattered Dreams: The Story of Mary Todd Lincoln* (Morgan Reynolds Inc., Greensboro, NC, 1994), 15.

p.68   "only a select class of lady patients . . ." Neely and McMurtry, 38.

p.69   "If she is only permitted . . ." Neely and McMurtry, 53.

p.69   "MRS. LINCOLN IS THE WIDOW . . ." Neely and McMurtry, 53-54.

p.70   "It struck me as being rather strange . . ." Friedman, 54

p.70   "assume any responsibility." Neely and McMurtry, 63-64.

p.73   "The constant excitement . . ." Neely and McMurtry, 63.

p.73   "REASON RESTORED . . ." Holmes, 730.

p.76   ". . . I have not at any time . . ." Friedman, 61.

p.76   "NOT THE SLIGHTEST TRACE . . ." Friedman, 65.

Chapter Nine—Last Years

p.80   "Mistress Lockwood, you are a woman." Friedman, 137.

p.80   "law of nature . . ." Friedman, 147.

p.86   "We are pleased to say . . ." CLN, April 5, 1890, 265.

Bibliography

Blockson, Charles L. *The Underground Railroad*. New York: Prentice Hall Press, 1987.

Collins, David R. *Shattered Dreams: The Story of Mary Todd Lincoln*. Greensboro, NC: Morgan Reynolds, Inc., 1994.

Friedman, Jane M. *America's First Woman Lawyer: The Biography of Myra Bradwell*. Buffalo, NY: Prometheus Books, 1993.

Howard, Robert P. *Illinois: A History of the Prairie State*. Grand Rapids, MI: William B. Eerdmans Publishing Co., 1972.

Keiser, John H. *Building for the Centuries: Illinois, 1865 to 1898*. Urbana, IL: University of Illinois Press, 1977.

Magdol, Edward. *Owen Lovejoy: Abolitionist in Congress*. New Brunswick, NJ: Rutgers University Press, 1967.

Muelder, Hermann R. *Fighters for Freedom: The History of Anti-Slavery Activities of Men and Women Associated with Knox College*. New York: Columbia University Press, 1959.

Nash, Gary B. and Jeffrey, Julie Roy, eds. *The American People: Creating a Nation and a Society. Vol. I*. 2nd Ed. New York: Harper & Row, 1990

Neely, Mark E. and McMurtry, R. Gerald. *The Insanity File: The Case of Mary Todd Lincoln*. Carbondale, IL: Southern Illinois University Press, 1986.

Simon, Paul. *Freedom's Champion: Elijah Lovejoy*. Carbondale and Edwardsville, IL: Southern Illinois University Press, 1994.

Index

Packard, Reverend Theophilus, 61
Palmer, Governor John, 36, 49, 50, 55
Patterson, Dr. Richard, 69-72, 74, 76-77
polygamy, 26

Reports of the Decision of the Appellate Court of the State of Illinois: 1871-1887, 79
Revised Statutes of the State of Illinois, 78
Rush Medical College, 26
Ryan, Chief Justice, 80, 82

Sandburg, Carl, 48
Stanton, Elizabeth Cady, 28, 34
Swett, Leonard, 66-67

The Nation, 56

U.S. Supreme Court, 9, 40, 87
Underground Railroad, 11-12

Voice of the Fair, 23

Waite, Catharine, 26, 28, 33-34, 53, 56
Waite, Charles, 26, 28, 33-35
Western Citizen, 12
Wheaton, Mrs. Dr., 35
Wilkie, Franc B., 71-72, 74